Try these -up popcorn recipes!

- ★Hot Cheese Popcorn
- ★Popcorn à la Rum
- ★Popcorn Nacho Dip
- ★Sweet and Sour Popcorn
- ★Popcorn-Pecan Stuffing
- ★Zucchini-Popcorn Lasagna
- ★Mediterranean Popcorn
- ★Popcorn-Stuffed Mushrooms

- ★Pastrami-Popcorn Cheeseball
- ★Popcorn Tacos
- ★Chocolate-Covered Popcorn
- ★Popcorn-Apple Cobbler
- ★Popcorn, Cheese, and Corn Soufflé
- ★Popcorn-Fudge Rocky Road
- ★Popcorn Clusters

...and more!

BANG!

The Explosive Popcorn Recipe Book

Robert T. Brucken

BALLANTINE BOOKS • NEW YORK

For Mickey and Alix

CONTENTS

BANG! UP POPCORNS

BANG! MAIN DISHES   59

BREAKFASTS WITH BANG!   77

BANG! BREADS, MUFFINS, ROLLS   87

INTRODUCTION

Popcorn is literally "exploding." Everyone is realizing that popcorn not only tastes good; it's good for your health. In fact, the Illinois division of the American Cancer Society recently listed popcorn as one of the "eleven things that don't cause cancer." Among others: a good laugh, exercise, fruit, and vegetables.

It's been recommended by the American Dental Association for sugar-free snacking, and nutritionists say that two cups of popcorn have about the same amount of calories as a medium-sized apple.

Few foods are as simple, versatile, or enjoyable as popcorn. From movie houses to sporting events to your own kitchen, no food is more fun, and that is what this book is all about: the joy of popcorn.

If you usually serve popcorn only one way—with butter and salt—you're in for a big surprise. Popcorn takes to flavors, spices, and seasonings like any good food. Like pizza? You'll like pizza popcorn. In fact you can even use popcorn flour to make pizza dough!

I wrote *BANG!* because I love popcorn and have been experimenting with hundreds of ways to prepare it over the years. The recipes that follow are those I consider the two hundred best: kitchen tested and uniformly delicious. You may wish to try an entire meal using popcorn for everything from appetizers to the dessert.

Popcorn can also provide the fixings for large parties because it is economical as well as delicious.

I honestly believe popcorn is a food without fault. It's healthy, tasty, low cost, low calorie, easy to store, easy to make, and everyone likes it. Few foods have all these qualities.

I love popcorn and I suspect you do too. I hope my book opens up even more ideas for you. Enjoy!

ROBERT BRUCKEN

FUNDAMENTALS

STORING POPCORN:
WHAT TO DO WITH WHAT YOU POP

One of popcorn's greatest virtues is its ability to keep. Air-popped popcorn will remain fresh for ninety days because it has no oil to make it stale. Keep it airtight in a plastic bag or container.

You should also store unpopped kernels in an airtight container to lock in the moisture. I buy the cheapest popcorn I can find at the market, add a couple of teaspoons of water per one-pound bag, shake it up, and let it sit until I need it. Popcorn kernels explode when the water in the kernel turns to steam. When you add these few drops of water to the kernels, you're essentially making your own gourmet popcorn!

I also enjoy popcorn the old-fashioned oil-popped way, just like my mother always made it. You can use regular cooking oil, flavored oil, or any grease or fat. They each add their own flavor to the kernel. Oil-popped corn should be used immediately or within three or four days if it's covered tightly.

HOW TO POP POPCORN

POPPING WITH OIL

Most cooking oils are fine to use. The most common are corn, peanut, vegetable, and coconut oil. There are also oils with flavors made just for popcorn popping.

Pour about ¼ cup of your favorite oil into a deep saucepan. Place on high heat on your stove. Pour in the kernels—about ⅔ cup—and wait for the oil to sizzle or reach 300° F. That's when kernels start to pop. Put a lid on the pan and shake gently so all kernels are covered with hot oil. As the temperature rises to 400° to 480° F the corn will pop better. The higher the temperature, the better the popcorn. You must keep shaking the pan so the popcorn and unpopped kernels don't burn. When popping slows down, get ready to pour into a bowl.

POPPING WITH AIR

Popping with air poppers is easy. Just follow directions on popper for correct measure of kernels. Release kernels into heat area, usually by way of a dumper that holds one batch of kernels. The air popper rotates and heats to the correct temperature. No shaking. Just place a bowl under the spout. Air poppers use no oil, so the popcorn stays fresher longer.

HOW TO MAKE POPCORN FLOUR

Popcorn flour is one of the true undiscovered pleasures of popcorn. Popcorn flour gives baked goods a nutlike flavor, and it can be combined with your regular flour for added taste.

To make popcorn flour, I use my kitchen blender. Just throw a couple of handfuls of popped corn in and set to chop or purée, for a coarse blend that's ideal for cookies and cakes. Grind it a little longer and it will become a finer flour for baking and cooking.

BUTTERS

Melt the amount of butter suggested for each recipe over low heat, being careful that it doesn't burn. Then stir in the seasonings. Each recipe will amply cover eight cups of popped corn.

BEST BUTTER

Melt 3 tablespoons butter over low heat. Stir in butter-flavored salt or popcorn seasoning. Drizzle over popcorn. Pepper to taste. Mix well.

ONION BUTTER

Melt 3 tablespoons butter over low heat. Dissolve one cube vegetable bouillon in butter. Drizzle over popcorn. Lightly sprinkle onion salt. Mix well.

SOUTHERN CHICKEN BUTTER

Melt 3 tablespoons butter over low heat. Dissolve 1 chicken bouillon cube in butter. Drizzle over popcorn. Mix well.

TEXAS BUTTER

Melt 3 tablespoons butter over low heat. Dissolve 1 beef bouillon cube in butter. Drizzle over popcorn. Mix well.

PEANUT–PEANUT BUTTER BUTTER

Melt 3 tablespoons butter over low heat. Add 3 tablespoons chunky peanut butter. Stir over low heat 4 to 5 minutes. Drizzle over popcorn. Add a handful of peanuts and lightly salt. Mix well.

MUSHROOM BUTTER

Melt 4 tablespoons butter over low heat. Add 3 tablespoons finely chopped fresh mushrooms and sauté over low heat for 5 minutes. Drizzle over popcorn and salt and pepper to taste. Mix well.

SOUTHERN CALIFORNIA BUTTER

Melt 3 tablespoons butter over low heat. Add 2 small dried red chili peppers and stir 5 minutes over low heat in covered pan. Remove chilies. Drizzle over popcorn. Sprinkle garlic salt to taste and add a pinch of pepper. Mix well.

HILLBILLY BUTTER

Melt 5 tablespoons butter over low heat. Add 3 chopped pieces of beef jerky, 1 teaspoon dried parsley flakes, and a pinch of oregano. Stir over low heat for 5 minutes. Drizzle over popcorn. Sprinkle salt and pepper to taste. Mix well.

HERB BUTTER 1

Melt 4 tablespoons butter over low heat. Add 1 teaspoon oregano, 1 teaspoon dried parsley, 1 teaspoon chopped chives, ½ teaspoon grated lemon rind. Stir over low heat for 4 minutes. Drizzle over popcorn. Sprinkle salt and pepper to taste. Mix well.

HERB BUTTER 2

Melt 4 tablespoons butter over low heat. Add ½ teaspoon paprika, ¼ teaspoon dry mustard, 2 tablespoons dried parsley, 1 tablespoon minced thyme. Stir over low heat 2 to 3 minutes. Drizzle over popcorn. Sprinkle salt and pepper to taste. Mix well.

HERB BUTTER 3

Melt 4 tablespoons butter over low heat. Add 1 teaspoon chopped parsley, 1 teaspoon chopped chives, a drop of lemon juice, 1 teaspoon celery seeds, and ¼ teaspoon each of oregano, thyme, basil, and rosemary. Stir over low heat. Drizzle over popcorn. Sprinkle salt and pepper to taste. Mix well.

PICKLE BUTTER

Melt 4 tablespoons butter over low heat. Add 1 teaspoon lemon juice, ¼ teaspoon dill, ¼ teaspoon thyme, and ½ teaspoon cider vinegar. Stir over low heat for 4 to 5 minutes. Drizzle over popcorn. Sprinkle salt and pepper to taste. Mix well.

ORANGE BUTTER

Melt 5 tablespoons butter over low heat. Add 3 teaspoons grated orange peel, ½ teaspoon almond extract, ½ teaspoon vanilla extract. Stir over low heat 4 to 5 minutes. Drizzle over popcorn. Salt lightly. Mix well.

ITALIAN BUTTER

Melt 3 tablespoons butter over low heat. Add one chopped garlic clove and stir over low heat 4 to 5 minutes. Drizzle over popcorn. Sprinkle garlic salt to taste. Mix well.

MEXICAN BUTTER

Melt 4 tablespoons butter over low heat. Add 1½ teaspoons dry taco seasoning mix. Lightly sprinkle onion salt. Mix well.

CHINESE SWEET AND SOUR BUTTER

Melt 3 tablespoons butter over low heat. Add ¼ tablespoon brown sugar, a dash of soy sauce, and a dash of cider vinegar. Stir together and drizzle over popcorn. Sprinkle onion salt. Mix well.

CHEESY ITALIAN BUTTER

Melt 5 tablespoons butter over low heat. Add 5 tablespoons grated Parmesan or Romano cheese and stir over low heat 2 to 3 minutes. Drizzle over popcorn. Lightly sprinkle onion salt and a little pepper over popcorn and shake on more Parmesan cheese. Mix well.

FRENCH BUTTER

Melt 5 tablespoons butter over low heat. Add 1 teaspoon lemon juice, 1 teaspoon parsley flakes, 1 teaspoon basil, and 2 teaspoons fresh chopped chives. Stir over low heat 4 to 5 minutes. Drizzle over popcorn. Add onion salt and pepper to taste. Mix well.

HOT GREEK BUTTER

Melt 4 tablespoons butter over low heat. Add 1 tablespoon fresh chopped chives, 1 bay leaf, 1 teaspoon lemon juice, and ¼ teaspoon cayenne pepper. Stir over low heat for 5 minutes. Remove bay leaf. Drizzle over popcorn. Lightly sprinkle garlic salt to taste. Mix well.

POLISH BUTTER

Melt 5 tablespoons butter over low heat. Add 2 ounces of chopped precooked Polish sausage. Stir over low heat for 5 minutes. Drizzle over popcorn. Sprinkle salt and pepper to taste. Mix well.

BANG!

UP

POPCORNS

In the following recipes, melted butter and toppings are to be mixed with 8 cups of popcorn.

STAY YOUNG POPCORN

Melt 5 tablespoons butter over low heat. Add 1 teaspoon ground millet and stir 1 to 2 minutes over low heat. Drizzle over popcorn. Sprinkle hulled sunflower seeds and sesame seeds. Lightly salt and pepper to taste. Mix well.

MEDITERRANEAN POPCORN

Melt 5 tablespoons butter over low heat. Stir in 1 crushed clove garlic, 1 teaspoon lemon juice, and 1 teaspoon chopped chives. Drizzle over popcorn. Sprinkle finely crumbled feta cheese and a few finely chopped drained black olives. Add onion salt. Mix well.

LICORICE POPCORN

Melt 4 tablespoons butter over low heat. Add 1 tablespoon anise extract and stir over low heat 4 to 5 minutes. Drizzle over popcorn. Add salt and pepper to taste. Mix well.

HOT CHEESE POPCORN

Melt 4 tablespoons butter over low heat. Add ½ cup finely grated sharp cheddar cheese and stir over low heat 2–3 minutes, or until melted. Stir in ½ teaspoon cayenne pepper and one pinch chili powder. Drizzle over popcorn. Add salt and pepper to taste. Mix well.

ONION POPCORN

Melt ½ cup butter over low heat. Add 1 teaspoon lemon juice, ¼ cup finely chopped onions, and ¼ cup dried parsley flakes. Stir over low heat 4 to 5 minutes. Drizzle over popcorn and lightly salt and pepper to taste. Onion salt may be used. Mix well.

ANCHOVY POPCORN

Melt 5 tablespoons butter over low heat. Add 1 tablespoon dried parsley flakes, 2 tablespoons chopped chives, and 1 tablespoon anchovy paste. Stir over low heat 4 to 5 minutes. Drizzle over popcorn. Add black pepper to taste. Mix well.

THOUSAND ISLAND POPCORN

Melt 5 tablespoons butter over low heat. Add 1 teaspoon celery seeds, ¼ teaspoon paprika, ½ teaspoon chili powder, ½ teaspoon cider vinegar, and 1 tablespoon chopped chives. Stir over low heat 4 to 5 minutes. Drizzle over popcorn and add salt and pepper to taste. Mix well.

POPCORN À LA RUM

Melt 4 tablespoons butter over low heat. Add 1 teaspoon rum extract and 2 tablespoons grated, chopped orange peel. Stir over low heat 4 to 5 minutes. Drizzle over popcorn and lightly salt and pepper to taste. Mix well.

CHEDDAR POPCORN

Melt 5 tablespoons butter over low heat. Add 1 teaspoon chopped chives, ¼ teaspoon paprika, 1 tablespoon finely chopped black olives, 5 tablespoons grated Cheddar cheese, and ½ cup crumbled bacon. Stir over low heat 4 to 5 minutes. Drizzle over popcorn. Add salt and pepper to taste. Mix well.

DATE-NUT POPCORN

Melt 4 tablespoons butter over low heat. Add 1 tablespoon brown sugar. Stir over low heat 2 to 3 minutes. Drizzle over popcorn. Sprinkle ½ cup finely chopped dates and ½ cup broken walnuts, pecans, or almonds. Lightly salt and pepper. Mix well.

NUT CRUMB POPCORN

Melt 4 tablespoons butter over low heat. Drizzle over popcorn. Stir in 2 cups broken vanilla wafers and ½ cup finely chopped nuts. Add salt and pepper to taste. Mix well.

THE TROPICS POPCORN

Melt 4 tablespoons butter over low heat. Stir in ½ teaspoon lemon or lime juice. Drizzle over popcorn. Sprinkle ½ cup shredded coconut, 2 tablespoons finely grated orange peel, and 1 cup dried whole banana chips. Add salt and pepper to taste. Mix well.

POPCORN CHEX

Melt 4 tablespoons butter over low heat. Stir in ½ teaspoon vanilla and a few pinches nutmeg. Drizzle over popcorn. Add 2 cups Rice Chex cereal and lightly sprinkle with powdered sugar. Mix well.

SWEET AND SOUR POPCORN

Melt 4 tablespoons butter over low heat. Add ¼ teaspoon Accent seasoning, 2 teaspoons chopped chives, and a pinch pepper. Stir over low heat 2 to 3 minutes. Drizzle over popcorn. Sprinkle 4 strips crumbled bacon. Salt and pepper to taste and lightly spray with vinegar. Mix well.

SPICY AND FRENCH POPCORN

Melt 4 tablespoons butter over low heat. Add 1 teaspoon chopped chives, 1 teaspoon dried parsley flakes, and ½ teaspoon paprika. Stir in and drizzle over popcorn. Add 2 cups croutons. Season with garlic powder, salt, and pepper. Mix well.

CURRY POPCORN

Melt 4 tablespoons butter over low heat. Add 1 teaspoon chopped parsley, 1 teaspoon curry powder, a drop of lemon juice, and two drops of Worcestershire sauce. Stir over low heat for 2 minutes. Drizzle over popcorn. Add a bit more curry powder with salt and pepper to taste. Mix well.

MARIGOLD POPCORN

Melt 4 tablespoons butter over low heat. Add 2 tablespoons marigold petals. Stir in and drizzle over popcorn. Sprinkle a few petals over popcorn mixture. Lightly salt. Mix well.

CHEESE AND BACON POPCORN

Melt 4 tablespoons butter over low heat. Drizzle over popcorn. Sprinkle 2 cups grated Cheddar cheese. Mix and place in warm oven to melt cheese. Remove from oven. Mix again to spread melted cheese evenly. Sprinkle 4 strips crumbled bacon. Lightly salt and pepper to taste. Mix well.

BIG BANANA POPCORN

Melt 4 tablespoons butter over low heat. Stir in 1 teaspoon vanilla extract. Drizzle over popcorn. Sprinkle ½ cup chopped nuts and ½ cup dried banana chips. Lightly salt. Mix well.

SUPER ORANGE-COCONUT POPCORN

Melt 5 tablespoons butter over low heat. Add 2 teaspoons grated orange peel, ½ teaspoon almond extract, and ½ teaspoon vanilla extract. Stir over low heat 4 to 5 minutes. Do not let butter turn brown. Drizzle over popcorn. Sprinkle grated coconut, 1 tablespoon finely grated orange peel, and a handful of toasted almonds. Mix well.

MINT BUTTER POPCORN

Melt 4 tablespoons butter over low heat. Add 2 tablespoons finely chopped fresh spearmint or 2 teaspoons mint extract. Stir over low heat for 4 to 5 minutes. Drizzle over popcorn. Lightly salt. Mix well.

LEMON POPCORN

Melt 4 tablespoons butter over low heat. Stir in 1 tablespoon lemon juice and a pinch of cayenne pepper over low heat and add ½ teaspoon grated lemon rind. Let simmer 1 to 2 minutes. Drizzle over popcorn and salt lightly. Mix well.

POPCORN LEMONADE

Melt 3 tablespoons butter over low heat. Stir in 1¼ teaspoons unsweetened dry lemonade mix and 1 tablespoon finely grated lemon. Drizzle over popcorn. Mix well.

TEA FOR TWO POPCORN

Melt 3 tablespoons butter over low heat. Stir in 2 teaspoons finely grated lemon peel. Sprinkle mixture with 2 tablespoons instant tea mix. Let simmer for 1 to 2 minutes and drizzle over popcorn. Salt and pepper to taste.

SPROUTS AND PARSLEY POPCORN

Melt 3 tablespoons butter over low heat. Add 3 tablespoons dried parsley flakes. Stir over low heat for 1 to 2 minutes. Drizzle over popcorn. Rinse 2 cups sprouts, drain and pat dry with paper towels. Sprinkle over popcorn. Salt and pepper to taste. Mix well.

POPCORN BACON

Melt 1 tablespoon butter over low heat. Fry 4 to 5 bacon strips over medium heat, drain and cool. Combine 2 tablespoons bacon grease with butter and drizzle over popcorn. Crumble bacon and sprinkle over popcorn with salt and pepper to taste. Mix well.

POPCORN SMOKIES

Melt 3 tablespoons butter over low heat. Drizzle over popcorn. Sprinkle on 3 finely chopped smokies (cooked and smoked sausage or beef jerky). Place in a 350° oven for five minutes. Remove and dot with 3 tablespoons brown mustard (prepared). Sprinkle 3 tablespoons grated Parmesan cheese. Return to oven for a few minutes. Remove and lightly sprinkle with onion salt and pepper to taste. Mix well.

CRABMEAT AND SHRIMP POPCORN

Melt 4 tablespoons butter over low heat. Add 2 tablespoons shredded shrimp and 2 tablespoons flaked crabmeat. Stir over low heat 4 to 5 minutes. Drizzle over popcorn. Sprinkle 3 more tablespoons shrimp plus 3 tablespoons flaked crabmeat. Lightly salt and mix well.

DIPS

POPCORN-TUNA-CHEESEBALL DIP

POPCORN: 1 cup coarsely ground

Mix together one 6½-ounce can drained tuna, one 3-ounce package cream cheese and 1 finely chopped medium onion. Mix in 2 tablespoons dried parsley flakes and 2 tablespoons finely chopped nuts. Chill, then shape into ball. Roll the ball in coarsely ground popcorn and serve with your favorite crackers or snacks.

POPCORN NACHO DIP

POPCORN: ½ cup finely ground

Brown ½ pound sausage, ½ pound ground beef, 1 large onion, chopped, and ½ cup finely ground popcorn, mixed together. When brown, remove excess fat and add 4 drops hot pepper sauce and 2 pinches of salt. Heat 2 cans refried beans. Stir well. Pour over meat mixture. Then cover with 3 cups grated Cheddar cheese. Drizzle ¾ cup taco sauce on top. Bake at 400° F for 20 minutes. Remove and serve with large bowl of popcorn and taco chips.

CUCUMBER-POPCORN-YOGURT DIP

POPCORN: ½ cup finely ground

Mix together thoroughly 1 cup plain yogurt, 1 cup cucumber salad dressing, 1 small onion, finely chopped, 1 teaspoon dried dill weed, 1 teaspoon vinegar, and ½ cup finely ground popcorn. Cool in refrigerator until ready to serve.

COLD MOON POPCORN DIP

POPCORN: 1 cup finely ground

Mix together ½ pint sour cream, 2 tablespoons finely chopped onion, 1 tablespoon dried parsley flakes, 1 teaspoon lemon juice, pinch of salt, and 1 cup finely ground popped popcorn. Spread on crackers or dip vegetable slices in mixture.

POPCORN-CAULIFLOWER SPREAD

POPCORN: 1 cup coarsely ground

Mix together 1 cup coarsely ground popcorn, ½ cup finely chopped pickled cauliflower, and 1 cup cream cheese. Spread on crackers or celery.

PASTRAMI-POPCORN CHEESEBALL

POPCORN: ½ cup coarsely ground

Mix one 8-ounce package cream cheese, 3 ounces diced pastrami, 3 medium-sized green onions, chopped, and 2 pinches of garlic salt. Form into ball and roll in coarsely ground popcorn. Garnish and serve for cracker spread.

BANG!

SOUPS

POPCORN-VEGETABLE CREAM SOUP

POPCORN: 2 tablespoons finely ground and ½ cup for topping

Sauté a small minced onion in 3 tablespoons butter, but do not brown onion. Add 2 tablespoons finely ground popcorn, 2½ tablespoons flour, pinch of salt, and pinch of paprika. Stir until smooth. Stir in 2 cups half-and-half and 2 cups beef or chicken broth. Simmer until thickened. Add 2 cups canned and drained succotash. Heat 4 to 5 more minutes and serve with a sprinkle of popcorn on top. Serves 6.

POTATO-POPCORN SOUP

POPCORN: 2 tablespoons finely ground and ½ cup for topping

Sauté minced onion in 3 tablespoons butter but do not brown onion. Transfer onion to top of double boiler over hot water. Add 8 cups milk and 4 cups mashed potatoes. Mix until smooth, then add 4 tablespoons finely ground popcorn and 2 tablespoons flour. Mix well until smooth. Do not boil mixture. Serve hot, topping each bowl with a pinch of parsley. Sprinkle with chives and float popcorn on top. Salt and pepper to taste. Serves 12.

POPCORN—PEANUT BUTTER SOUP

POPCORN: 4 tablespoons coarsely ground and ½ cup for topping

Melt 3 tablespoons butter in a 2-quart saucepan. Add one small onion, minced. Mix in 4 tablespoons coarsely ground popcorn, cup peanut butter, 4 cups chicken broth, and pinch of pepper. Stir on low heat until thick and smooth. Serve hot, topping off each bowl with a tablespoon of whipped cream and a sprinkling of popcorn. Serves 5 to 6.

CORNEY POPCORN DUMPLINGS

POPCORN: ½ cup coarsely ground

Mix 2 cups cornmeal, 3 pinches of salt, and 2 table-spoons brewer's yeast. Add 1 egg and blend in enough hot beef or chicken broth to make thick paste. Shape into dumplings and roll in ½ cup flour and ½ cup coarsely ground popcorn mixture. Drop into your favorite soup, cover, and simmer 10 to 12 minutes.

POPCORN-CURRY SOUP BALLS

POPCORN: ¼ cup finely ground

Mix together 1 cup soft wheat bread crumbs and ¼ cup finely ground popcorn, 2½ tablespoons butter, 1 grated hard-boiled egg, 1 raw egg yolk, and ½ teaspoon curry powder. Mix and shape into small balls. Drop into your favorite hot soup or broth. Cook for 5 minutes and serve.

SIDE DISHES

POPCORN BROCCOLI

POPCORN: 4 cups

Mix ½ cup melted butter, 6 ounces shredded jalapeño cheese, and 1 can cream of mushroom soup. Add 1 package chopped broccoli, cooked. Mix together and simmer 2 to 3 minutes over low heat. Fill small cereal bowls with popped popcorn, drizzle mixture over top, and serve. Serves 6.

POTATOES À LA POPCORN

POPCORN: 6 tablespoons finely ground

Bake 4 medium potatoes. Slice potatoes in half and scoop out insides, preserving skins. Mash potatoes, adding 6 tablespoons finely ground popcorn, ¼ teaspoon salt, and 5 tablespoons finely grated sharp Cheddar cheese. Fill potato skins with mixture and bake for 10 to 12 minutes at 350° F. Lightly salt, pepper, and butter. Serves 8.

POPCORN-STUFFED MUSHROOMS

POPCORN: 1½ cups finely ground

Remove stems from 20 mushrooms and finely chop the stems only. Pan-fry 4 to 5 slices of bacon until crisp. Drain on paper towels. In the same pan keep 2 tablespoons of bacon fat and cook 2 tablespoons of chopped green pepper, the mushroom stems, and 1 finely chopped small onion. Cook about 2 minutes or until tender. Add 1½ cups finely ground popcorn, 1 teaspoon seasoned salt, and pinch of pepper. Stuff mushroom caps with mixture and place in a shallow buttered baking dish in 350° F oven for 20 minutes. Serves 4.

POPCORN HASH

POPCORN: 1 cup coarsely ground

Mix together 4 cooked potatoes, cut up, 4 chopped small onions, 1 can corned beef (not hash), and 1 cup coarsely ground popcorn. Mix with salt and pepper to taste and serve on lettuce leaf. Serves 6.

POPCORN-APPLE CASSEROLE

POPCORN: ¼ cup coarsely ground

Combine 1 cup dry bread crumbs and ¼ cup coarsely ground popcorn in ⅓ cup melted butter. Mix well. Use ⅓ of the mixture to cover bottom of baking dish. Mix together ¾ cup brown sugar, 1 teaspoon cinnamon, a pinch of nutmeg, a pinch of cloves, and 1 teaspoon vanilla. Peel and slice 2½ cups apples and place ½ of the sliced apples over popcorn mixture in dish. Sprinkle with ½ of sugar mixture, adding 2 tablespoons water. Sprinkle second third of popcorn mixture. Add remaining apples and 2 tablespoons water. Drizzle 4 tablespoons lemon juice and top off with rest of popcorn mixture. Cover the dish and bake at 350° F for about 40 minutes. Remove cover and bake 15 more minutes. Serves 6.

POPCORN BREAD PUDDING

POPCORN: 2 cups coarsely ground

Mix 2 cups milk, 2 cups bread crumbs, 2 cups coarsely ground popcorn, ¼ cup soften butter, 2 beaten eggs, ½ cup sugar, ½ teaspoon salt, 1 teaspoon cinnamon, and ½ cup raisins. Place in buttered baking dish, dot with a little butter, and bake at 350° F for 45 minutes. Serves 4.

POPCORN CREPES

POPCORN: ¼ cup finely ground, ½ cup coarsely ground, and a few popped kernels for topping

Mix 2 eggs, ¾ cup flour, ¼ cup finely ground popcorn, and 1 cup milk until smooth and soupy. Pour enough batter into hot, greased frying pan to get desired sized crepes. Keep them thin and round, shaping them with a spoon. Turn and brown other side. When finished, stuff and roll with your favorite jelly, marmalade, or cream cheese mixed with coarsely ground popcorn and top with powdered sugar and a few kernels of popcorn. Serves about 6.

POPCORN QUICHE FILLING

POPCORN: 1 tablespoon finely ground

Mix until smooth 1 tablespoon finely ground popcorn, 1¾ tablespoons flour, and 1 cup milk, 2 eggs,
and 1 teaspoon vanilla. Add 1 cup grated Cheddar
cheese, pinch of salt, a few raisins or chopped dates,
and mix well. Pour this mixture into unbaked tart
shells and cook at 350° F for about 35 minutes, or
until eggs are set.

CORDON BLEU POPCORN

POPCORN: 4 cups

Fill pie dish with popcorn. Melt 3 tablespoons butter
and stir in 1 teaspoon onion powder and 1 teaspoon
dried parsley flakes. Drizzle over popcorn and mix.
On top of popcorn place slices of Swiss cheese to
cover. Place in 250° F oven until cheese is melted
(about 10 minutes). Lightly salt and pepper to taste.

POPCORN FRUIT SALAD

POPCORN: 3 cups

Mix 1 can drained mandarin orange sections, 1 bunch green grapes, 3 sliced bananas, 2 chopped apples, and a cup of blueberries. Toss with a little powdered sugar and chill. Before serving, mix in 3 cups popcorn. Serves 8.

POPCORN AND RED KIDNEY BEAN SALAD

POPCORN: 1 cup coarsely ground

Mix 1 can drained red kidney beans, 1 finely chopped medium onion, 3 chopped hard-boiled eggs, ⅓ cup mayonnaise, and dash of pepper and salt. Mix well and chill. Before serving, mix in 1 cup coarsely ground popcorn. Serve on a lettuce leaf. Serves 4.

POPCORN–COTTAGE CHEESE– BANANA SALAD

POPCORN: ¾ cup coarsely ground

Slice 4 bananas in bowl. Add 1½ cups cottage cheese, ½ cup raisins, and 2 tablespoons mayonnaise. Mix well. Place in serving bowl and sprinkle with ¾ cup coarsely ground popcorn. Serves 4.

POPCORN MEXICAN SALAD

POPCORN: 4 cups

Brown and drain 1 pound ground beef. In large bowl, combine beef, 8 ounces grated Cheddar cheese, and 4 cups of popcorn. Mix well. Add 1 shredded small head of lettuce, ¼ teaspoon cayenne pepper, ½ teaspoon chili powder, ½ teaspoon ground cumin seed, 1 chopped green pepper, 1 chopped medium onion, 3 sliced medium carrots, and 1 large tomato cut in small wedges. Mix well and add ready-made seasoned salad dressing to taste. Serves 4.

POPCORN PLUS THREE BEAN SALAD

POPCORN: 2½ cups

Mix together 1 small can drained green beans, 1 small can drained garbanzo beans, and 1 small can drained kidney beans. Add 2 chopped small onions, 2 tablespoons parsley, and a pinch of garlic powder. Stir. Pour on Italian dressing and stir to coat. Refrigerate for 1 hour. Before serving stir in 2½ cups buttered popcorn. Serves 10.

POPCORN–TUNA SALAD SANDWICH

POPCORN: ½ cup coarsely ground

Mix 1 can drained tuna with 1 small chopped onion, 2 tablespoons pickle relish, and 1 chopped hard-cooked egg. Mix in 3 tablespoons mayonnaise and ½ cup coarsely ground popcorn. Spread on bread. Makes 4 sandwiches.

POPCORN AND BREAD STUFFING

POPCORN: 1½ cups coarsely ground

Sauté ½ cup chopped onion and 1 cup chopped celery in 3 tablespoons melted butter. Add to bowl with 3 cups bread crumbs and 1½ cups coarsely ground popcorn. Mix well. Add 3 tablespoons dried parsley, 1 teaspoon salt, 1 teaspoon sage or thyme, and a little water to moisten. Mix well. This mixture will stuff a 4- to 5-pound chicken or 6 pork chops.

POPCORN-PECAN STUFFING

POPCORN: 2 cups coarsely ground

Melt ⅓ cup butter and add ¾ cup chopped onion and ¾ cup chopped celery. Sauté until tender. Add 2 cups bread crumbs and 2 cups coarsely ground popcorn. Mix in 2 pinches of salt and pepper, pinch of sage, pinch of marjoram, pinch of thyme, ½ teaspoon dried parsley flakes, and ¾ cup chopped pecans. Moisten with ½ cup water and mix. Makes enough to stuff an 8- to 10-pound turkey or large chicken.

POPCORN PARTY MIX

POPCORN: 8 cups

Mix together in a pan 1 cup Cheerios, 2 cups small cheese-flavored crackers, 4 cups popcorn, 2 cups pretzel sticks, and ½ pound mixed nuts. Melt ⅓ cup butter, add ½ teaspoon Worcestershire sauce, and 2 dashes of garlic salt. Drizzle butter mixture over party mix and stir well. Bake in a 225° F oven for about ¾ hour. Stir regularly. Serves 10.

MAIN
DISHES

POPCORN-ZUCCHINI
STUFFED PEPPERS

POPCORN: 1 cup finely ground

Mix 1 pound ground beef, 1 small minced onion, 1 cup finely ground popcorn, ¾ cup shredded zucchini, 4 tablespoons of your favorite salad dressing, a pinch of cayenne pepper, 1 tablespoon dried parsley flakes, ½ teaspoon dried basil, and dash of salt and pepper. Cut 2 large green peppers in half lenghwise and remove seeds. Lightly salt green peppers. Stuff and bake at 325° F for 1 hour 20 minutes.

POPCORN GOULASH

POPCORN: 2 cups coarsely ground

Brown 1 pound ground beef, then drain. Add 1 cup chopped onion, a minced clove of garlic, and a pinch of salt. Stir in 2½ cups tomato juice, 2 cups beef or chicken broth, 2 teaspoons Worcestershire sauce, a pinch of celery salt, 2 cups coarsely ground popcorn, and ⅔ cup water. Mix together and pour over 4 cups cooked noodles. Cover and cook about 15 minutes. Serves 4.

POPCORN-COVERED FISH

POPCORN: ½ finely ground

Mix ½ cup finely ground popcorn and 1 cup all-purpose flour. Add 3 teaspoons baking powder and 2 pinches of salt. In separate bowl, beat well 1 egg; continue beating and add 1 cup cold water. Stir in to dry mixture, stirring until batter is smoother. Coat 4 medium-sized fish fillets in batter. Fry in hot oil (375° F) until golden brown.

POPCORN-CHICKEN CASSEROLE

POPCORN: ½ cup coarsely ground and 1 cup coarsely ground

Combine 2 cups diced cooked chicken, ½ teaspoon Worcestershire sauce, 1 can cream of chicken soup, undiluted, 1 cup shredded Swiss cheese, 1 small can drained peas. Transfer mixture into buttered casserole. Top with ½ cup coarsely ground popcorn and bake at 350° F for 35 minutes. Serve over bed of rice mixed in equal proportions with coarsely ground popcorn. Serves 6.

POPCORN–CORNED BEEF CASSEROLE

POPCORN: ¾ cup coarsely ground

Cook one 8-ounce package noodles in salt water until tender. Drain. In large bowl combine noodles with one 12-ounce can diced corned beef, ¼ pound grated Cheddar cheese, one 10½-ounce can cream of chicken soup, undiluted, 1 cup milk, and ½ cup diced onion. Transfer into greased 2-quart casserole. Top with ¾ cup coarsely ground popcorn. Bake in 350° F oven for 45 minutes. Serves 6.

POPCORN, BROWN RICE, AND NUTS CASSEROLE

POPCORN: 1 cup coarsely ground

Mix together 2 cups cooked brown rice, 2 cups grated Cheddar cheese, 1 cup grated Swiss cheese, 2 pinches of salt, 2 cups milk, 3 eggs, 1 medium chopped onion, 3 teaspoons dried parsley flakes, 1 cup coarsely ground popcorn, and ½ cup chopped nuts. Bake for 35 minutes at 350° F until brown. Serves 8.

POPCORN-MUSHROOM CASSEROLE

POPCORN: 2 tablespoons finely ground and ½ cup
coarsely ground

Sauté 1 pound whole mushrooms in butter. Dissolve
2 beef bouillon cubes in ½ cup water. Melt ¼ cup
butter and stir in 2 tablespoons finely ground popcorn. Add broth, ½ cup cream (half and half), and
pinch of salt and pepper. Place mushrooms in buttered baking dish and pour sauce over top. Sprinkle
½ cup coarsely ground popcorn and 1 cup Parmesan cheese. Bake at 350° F for about 30 minutes.
Serves 4.

ZUCCHINI-POPCORN LASAGNA

POPCORN: 2 tablespoons finely ground and ½ cup coarsely ground

Brown ½ pound ground beef. Add ⅓ cup chopped onion and cook onions until golden brown. Drain fat from beef and add one 16-ounce jar spaghetti sauce. In separate bowl, mix one 8-ounce container cottage cheese, 1 egg, ¼ teaspoon basil, and ⅓ cup Parmesan cheese. Grease baking dish and place a layer of thinly sliced zucchini on bottom (about 2 cups). Sprinkle with 2 tablespoons finely ground popcorn. Layer on ½ the cottage cheese mixture followed by ½ the meat mixture and repeat with remaining mixtures. Bake at 375° F for 20 minutes. Top with ½ cup coarsely ground popcorn and bake for 10 minutes longer.

POPCORN—COTTAGE CHEESE BAKE

POPCORN: 1 cup coarsely ground

Mix together 1 pound shredded brick cheese, 1 cup milk, 1 cup coarsely ground popcorn, 1 pint cottage cheese, 6 eggs slightly beaten, and ½ cup melted butter. Pour mixture into buttered baking dish and bake for 40 minutes at 375° F until golden. Serves 8 to 10.

POPCORN, CHEESE, AND CORN SOUFFLÉ

POPCORN: ½ tablespoon finely ground

Melt 2 tablespoons butter. Stir in 1½ tablespoons flour and ½ tablespoon finely ground popcorn. Mix until smooth. Add ½ cup milk and 1 cup grated Cheddar cheese. Cook, stirring, over low heat for 1 minute. Stir in 1 cup frozen or drained canned corn. Then add 3 egg yolks, a pinch each of salt, pepper, and tabasco. Cool. Fold in 3 stiffly beaten egg whites. Pour into greased casserole dish until ¾ full. Place in pan of hot water in 350° F oven and bake for about 20 minutes.

POPCORN MEATLOAF

POPCORN: 2 cups coarsely ground

Mix 1 pound ground beef and 1 pound ground pork, 2 cups coarsely ground popcorn, 1 tablespoon mayonnaise, 2 eggs, 1 tablespoon catsup, and 1 tablespoon mustard. Shape in a loaf pan and bake at 350° F for 1 hour or until brown. Serves 8 to 10.

POPCORN SWEDISH MEATBALLS

POPCORN: ¾ and ½ cup coarsely ground

Combine well 1½ pounds ground beef, ½ teaspoon salt, ½ teaspoon garlic salt, 1 teaspoon oregano, ⅓ cup Romano cheese, 1 egg, ½ teaspoon pepper, 1 small chopped onion, ¾ cup coarsely ground popcorn, and 1 cup milk. Shape into small balls and brown in ½ cup cooking oil. Place in a casserole. Mix ½ cup water, 1 can cream of mushroom soup, ½ cup coarsely ground popcorn and pour over meatballs in casserole. Bake in 325° F oven for 1 hour.

POPCORN ITALIAN MEATBALLS

POPCORN: 2 cups finely ground

Moisten and soften 2 cups finely ground popcorn for 2 minutes in 1½ cups water. Squeeze out water. Combine popcorn, 1 pound ground beef, 2 eggs, ½ cup grated Romano cheese, 2 tablespoons dried parsley flakes, 1 minced clove garlic, 1 teaspoon oregano, 2 pinches of salt, and pinch of pepper. Mix well and shape into small balls. Bake on cookie sheet in 350° F oven for about 7 to 10 minutes. Use as hors d'oeuvres or with spaghetti sauce.

POPCORN TACOS

POPCORN: 1½ cups coarsely ground

Brown 1 pound ground beef and drain off fat. Add pinch each of salt and pepper. Set aside. Chop one onion, shred ⅓ head lettuce, and chop 2 tomatoes. Shred ½ pound Cheddar cheese. Fill prepared taco shells in layers: a little meat, onions, coarsely ground popcorn, lettuce, tomato, and top with cheese and coarsely ground popcorn.

CROCK-POT POPCORN CHILI

POPCORN: 3 tablespoons finely ground and popped kernels for topping

Brown 1 pound ground beef, then drain off fat. Add ½ cup chopped onions and ¼ cup chopped green peppers. Simmer 5 minutes. Stir in 3 tablespoons finely ground popcorn, ½ teaspoon garlic powder, 1 tablespoon ground cumin, 1 tablespoon brown sugar, 2 pinches of salt. Put in slow cooker and add two 16-ounce cans hot chili beans and 4 cups chopped canned tomatoes. Simmer on low heat for 6 hours. Serve with a handful of whole popcorn on top of each bowlful.

POPCORN TORPEDO

POPCORN: 6 cups

Slice 1 loaf of French bread lengthwise and remove most of the soft bread with a fork. Place a layer of Swiss cheese on the inside of the bottom half. Place a layer of popcorn on top of cheese. Over low heat melt 5 tablespoons butter. Add 1 diced clove garlic, and 1 tablespoon chopped chives, and cook, stirring, 4 to 5 minutes. Drizzle over popcorn layer. Sprinkle Swiss cheese on top of popcorn. Put top half of loaf on top of bottom half. Place on cookie sheet and heat in a 250° oven until cheese is melted. Slice.

A main dish that everyone will like is breadless pizza. It requires no more than one large pizza pan, 6 cups of popcorn, and a soaring imagination. Here are five recipes for inspiration:

POPCORN PIZZA

POPCORN: 6 cups

Melt 3 tablespoons butter and drizzle over popcorn. Layer large pizza pan with buttered popcorn. Melt 4 tablespoons butter and ½ teaspoon of garlic powder over low heat. Remove from heat and drizzle over popcorn. Sprinkle 1½ cups grated Parmesan or mozzarella cheese over top of popcorn. Shake on some dried hot pepper flakes and place in oven at 250° F for 10 minutes. Remove and add salt and pepper to taste.

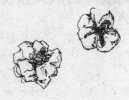

ANCHOVY-POPCORN PIZZA

POPCORN: 6 cups

Melt 3 tablespoons butter over low heat and drizzle over popcorn. Mix well. Spread popcorn over a large pizza pan. Sprinkle 3 tablespoons finely chopped onions, 1½ cups finely grated mozzarella cheese, 1 tablespoon dried parsley flakes, and 1 teaspoon chopped chili peppers. Top with ½ can flat anchovies, drained and finely chopped. Pepper and place in oven at low heat. Serve when cheese is melted.

ONION AND PEPPER–POPCORN PIZZA

POPCORN: 6 cups

Melt 3 tablespoons butter over low heat and drizzle over popcorn. Mix well. Spread popcorn over large pizza pan. Sprinkle 1 small can fried onion rings, 4 tablespoons finely chopped green pepper, 1½ cups finely grated mozzarella cheese, a pinch of basil, and a pinch of ground cayenne. Place in oven at low heat until cheese is melted.

MUSHROOM-POPCORN PIZZA

POPCORN: 6 cups

Melt 3 tablespoons butter over low heat and drizzle over popcorn. Mix well. Spread over large pizza pan. Drain and pat dry one small can mushroom slices. Sprinkle mushrooms, pinch each of onion, salt, and basil, and ½ cup grated mozzarella cheese. Add a pinch of ground cayenne. Place in oven at low heat until cheese is melted.

SAUSAGE-POPCORN PIZZA

POPCORN: 6 cups

Melt 3 tablespoons butter over low heat and drizzle over popcorn. Spread over large pizza pan. Sprinkle 1 cup finely chopped smokies or beef jerky, 1½ cups grated mozzarella cheese, 1 pinch each of basil, oregano, and hot pepper. Place in low-heat oven until cheese is melted.

BREAKFASTS
WITH
BANG!

POPCORN GRANOLA

POPCORN: 2 cups coarsely ground

Mix 2 cups coarsely ground popcorn, 4½ cups rolled oats, 1½ cups hulled sunflower seeds, ½ cup sesame seeds, ½ cup shredded coconut, ¼ cup wheat germ, and ½ cup chopped almonds. Drizzle over 3 tablespoons honey. Mix well. Spread out on 2 cookie sheets and bake at 350° F for 20 minutes. Make certain granola does not burn. Serve with milk as cereal.

POPCORN SUPREME GRANOLA

POPCORN: 2 cups coarsely ground

Mix together 2 cups oat flakes, 2 cups coarsely ground popcorn, ½ cup hulled sunflower seeds, ½ cup wheat germ, ½ cup chopped walnuts, ½ cup raisins, ½ cup chopped dried apples, ½ cup coconut, 3 tablespoons corn oil, 3 tablespoons wildflower honey, and 2 tablespoons molasses. Mix well and spread out on cookie sheet and bake at 350° F for 20 minutes. Serve with milk.

POPCORN-ALMOND-DATE GRANOLA

POPCORN: 2 cups coarsely ground

Mix together 2 cups oat flakes cereal, 2 cups coarsely ground popcorn, ½ cup slivered almonds, ½ cup finely chopped dates, 2 tablespoons maple syrup, and 2 tablespoons corn oil. Mix well and spread out on cookie sheet and bake at 350° F for 20 minutes. Serve with milk.

POPCORN-APPLE-SPICE GRANOLA

POPCORN: 1 cup coarsely ground

Mix together 1 cup oat flakes cereal, 1 cup coarsely ground popcorn, ½ cup wheat germ, ½ cup chopped dried apples, ½ cup blueberries, pinch of cinnamon, 2 tablespoons blackstrap molasses, 2 tablespoons corn oil, and 3 tablespoons wildflower honey. Mix well and spread out on cookie sheet and bake at 350° F for 20 minutes. Serve with milk.

HOT POPCORN CEREAL

POPCORN: 4½ cups coarsely ground

Scald 2 cups milk in saucepan. Add 4½ cups coarsely ground popcorn, 4 tablespoons wheat germ, and 2 tablespoons brown sugar. Let stand a few seconds and serve in cereal bowls with milk.

HONEY-COATED POPCORN AND FRUIT CEREAL

POPCORN: 8 cups

Mix 8 cups popcorn with 1 small package mixed dried fruit. Place in large, shallow baking pan and keep in 200° F oven. Bring 1 cup honey to a bubbly boil. Pour over warm popcorn and dried fruit mixture and stir until well coated. Let cool and store in airtight container. Serve in cereal bowls with milk.

NUTS AND POPCORN CEREAL

POPCORN: 8 cups

Melt 2½ tablespoons butter over low heat. Drizzle over 8 cups popcorn combined with 2 cups mixed nuts, crushed, and ½ cup wheat germ. Mix well. Serve in cereal bowls with milk.

POPCORN WAFFLES

POPCORN: ½ cup finely ground

Mix 1½ cups all-purpose flour, ½ cup finely ground popcorn, 3 teaspoons baking powder, and a pinch of salt. Beat 3 egg whites until stiff. Then add 3½ tablespoons sugar and continue beating, mixing well. Beat together 3 egg yolks, 1¾ cups milk, and ¼ cup melted shortening. Mix into flour mixture. Fold egg whites gently into mixture. It's ready for the griddle. Serve with corn syrup.

POPCORN AND CHEESE OMELET

POPCORN: 1 cup coarsely ground

Mix together 1 cup coarsely ground popcorn and ¼ cup milk. Let stand for about 5 minutes. Mix in 2 well-beaten eggs and a pinch of salt. Melt 1 tablespoon butter in omelet pan. Pour mixture into pan and cook over medium heat. Add such fillings as diced peppers, sliced cooked potatoes, crumbled bacon, or grated cheese. After adding filling, fold over and serve.

POPCORN-SAUSAGE BREAKFAST

POPCORN: 1½ cups finely ground

Mix together well 2 pounds ground pork sausage, 2 eggs, 2 tablespoons grated onion, 1½ cups finely ground popcorn, and ¼ cup chopped parsley. Pack into a loaf pan. Bake 20 minutes at 350° F. Remove and pour off excess fat. Return to oven for another 20 minutes. Remove and serve on large platter with scrambled eggs.

POPCORN-POTATO PANCAKES

POPCORN: 1 cup coarsely ground

Mix together 3 pounds diced cooked potatoes, 1 cup coarsely ground popcorn, 2 eggs, and a dash each of salt and pepper. Heat a well-greased frying pan and pour in pancake mixture. Fry until underside is golden brown, turn, adding oil as needed, and fry until second side is browned.

BANG!

BREADS, MUFFINS, ROLLS

POPCORN–PEANUT BUTTER–
BANANA BREAD

POPCORN: ½ cup finely ground

Mash 3 ripe bananas and stir in 1 cup sugar, 1 egg, ½ cup finely ground popcorn, 1 cup flour, ¼ cup soft butter, 1 teaspoon baking soda, 1 teaspoon salt, and ½ cup peanut butter. Pour into a buttered loaf pan and bake at 325° F for about 1 hour.

POPCORN CORN BREAD

POPCORN: 1 cup coarsely ground

Mix together ¾ cup flour, 1 teaspoon salt, 3½ teaspoons baking powder, 1 cup cornmeal, and 1 cup coarsely ground popcorn. In separate bowl mix 1 beaten egg, 1 cup milk, and ¼ cup softened butter. Add egg mixture to dry ingredients, mix together well, pour into greased dish, and bake at 425° F for 40 minutes.

BANANA-POPCORN BREAD

POPCORN: ½ cup finely ground

Cream together ½ cup shortening and 1 cup sugar. Add 2 eggs, 4 very ripe mashed bananas, ½ cup finely ground popcorn, 1½ cups flour, 1 teaspoon baking soda, and ½ cup chopped nuts. Pour into large loaf pan and bake in 350° F oven for 40 minutes.

POPCORN-PUMPKIN BREAD

POPCORN: ½ cup finely ground

In a large bowl mix together 1½ cups sugar, ½ cup finely ground popcorn, 1¼ cups flour, ½ cup canned pumpkin, ½ cup salad oil, ½ cup water, ¼ teaspoon vanilla, 1 egg, ¼ teaspoon baking powder, 2 pinches of salt, 1 teaspoon baking soda, ¼ teaspoon nutmeg, ¼ teaspoon cinnamon. Stir well and pour into a greased loaf pan. Bake in 325° F oven for about 1½ hours.

SHORT (POPCORN) BREAD

POPCORN: ½ cup finely ground

Cream together 4 tablespoons butter, ½ cup shortening, 3 tablespoons sugar. Stir in 1½ cups of flour, ½ cup of finely ground popcorn, and 1 cup flaked coconut. Divide dough in half. Shape into 2 loaves. Cover and chill. Then bake on a cookie sheet at 375° F for about 20 minutes. Pull out of oven and sprinkle with coarsely ground popcorn.

POPCORN MUFFINS

POPCORN: ½ cup finely ground

Beat 3 eggs well. Add ⅓ cup milk. Beat in 1½ cups wheat flour, ½ cup finely ground popcorn, ¾ cup sugar, 2 teaspoons baking powder, and a pinch of salt. Stir in ⅓ cup oil and 2 teaspoons grated orange rind. Spoon into greased muffin tins until ⅔ full. Bake at 350° F about 45 minutes. Serve hot with herb butter.

POPCORN BRAN MUFFINS WITH RAISINS

POPCORN: ½ cup coarsely ground

Cream together 1 tablespoon butter and ¼ cup sugar.
Dissolve 1 teaspoon baking soda in 1 cup buttermilk.
Stir in ¼ cup coarsely ground popcorn, ¼ cup flour,
2 cups bran flakes, ½ cup raisins, and 1 egg. Spoon
into muffin tins until ⅔ full. Bake in 400° F oven
for 20 minutes.

POPCORN–ICE CREAM MUFFINS

POPCORN: ¼ cup finely ground

Mix 1 cup softened ice cream (any flavor), ¼ cup
finely ground popcorn, and ¾ cup self-rising flour.
Pour into paper-lined muffin tins until ⅔ full. Place
in 400° F oven for 25 minutes. Cool and serve with
scoop of ice cream.

POPCORN DINNER ROLLS

POPCORN: 1⅔ cups finely ground

Mix ½ cup butter into 2 cups scalded milk, stirring until melted. Set aside to cool. In separate bowl dissolve 2 packages dry yeast in ½ cup warm water. Add to milk and butter mixture. Mix in 1½ teaspoons salt, ½ cup honey, and 2 eggs. Mix together well. Add 1⅔ cups finely ground popcorn, 5⅓ cups unbleached flour and mix. Dough should be sticky. Drop spoonfuls onto greased baking pan and let rise until double. Bake in 400° F oven for 10 minutes until brown. Remove and serve hot.

POPCORN CRESCENTS

POPCORN: 1 cup finely ground

Mix ½ cup butter into 1 cup scalded milk. Set aside to cool. In separate bowl dissolve 1 package dry yeast in ¼ cup warm water and add to milk mixture. Mix in 3 beaten eggs, ½ cup sugar, 1 teaspoon salt, 1 cup finely ground popcorn, and 3 cups flour. Let dough rise in warm place until double in bulk. Divide into thirds and roll out each into large circle ¼ inch thick. Coat with melted butter and slice into pie wedges. Let rise again until double in bulk. Place on greased cookie sheet and bake at 400° F for 10 to 15 minutes.

POPCORN BISCUITS

POPCORN: 1 cup finely ground

Mix together 1½ cups flour, 1 cup finely ground popcorn, 4 teaspoons baking powder, ¼ cup dry milk powder, and 2 pinches of salt. Blend in ⅓ cup shortening until mixture appears crumbly. Add ¾ cup milk and mix well. Knead on floured board about 12 minutes. Roll out to about 1 inch thick and cut with biscuit cutter. Place 2 inches apart on greased cookie sheet. Bake at 425° F for 12 to 15 minutes.

POPCORN BREAD PRETZELS

POPCORN: 1¼ cups finely ground

Mix 1¼ cups hot water with 1 package dry yeast and ½ teaspoon sugar. Let stand for one hour. Stir in 3¼ cups all-purpose flour and 1¼ cups finely ground popcorn. Knead dough for 7 or 8 minutes. Let dough rise in covered, greased bowl in warm place until double in bulk. Remove ½ cup and form into stick about 9 inches long and ¼ inch thick. Tie stick into a loop. Repeat with rest of dough. Place on greased cookie sheet. Paint tops with 1 egg yolk beaten with 2 tablespoons milk. Sprinkle with coarse salt. Cover pretzels and allow to rise again (not quite double). Bake in 475° F oven for about 10 minutes. Serve warm or cool.

DESSERTS

POPCORN CAKE

POPCORN: ¾ cup finely ground and enough for topping

Cream together 1 cup shortening and 2⅔ cups sugar. Add 1½ cups milk. Mix in 4¾ cups flour, ¾ cup finely ground popcorn, 5 teaspoons baking powder, and ½ teaspoon salt. Beat 6 egg whites and fold into mixture, adding 2 teaspoons vanilla. Pour into three greased 9-inch layer pans or 9 × 13–inch sheet cake pan. Bake 30 minutes in a preheated 375° F oven. Spread with your favorite frosting and top with popcorn.

POPCORN-YOGURT CAKE

POPCORN: ¾ cup finely ground and enough for topping

Mix together ¾ cup finely ground popcorn, 2¼ cups flour, and 1 teaspoon baking powder. Beat 3 eggs thoroughly and add to dry ingredients. Beat in 1 cup plain yogurt, 1 teaspoon vanilla, and ¾ cup corn oil. Pour into 8-inch baking dish and bake in a preheated 350° F oven for 50 minutes. Cool and refrigerate. Frost with your favorite flavor yogurt and sprinkle top with popcorn.

POPCORN-APPLE-MOLASSES CAKE

POPCORN: ½ cup finely ground

Slowly cook 1½ cups thinly sliced apples in ¾ cup molasses until tender. Set aside and cool. Melt ⅓ cup shortening in ½ cup hot water. Stir in 2 cups flour and ½ cup finely ground popcorn. Stir in molasses and apple mixture, pour into greased baking dish, and bake in a preheated 350° F oven for 30 minutes.

POPCORN SHORTCAKE

POPCORN: ½ cup finely ground

Mix together 1½ cups flour, ½ cup finely ground popcorn, 1 tablespoon baking powder, 3 tablespoons sugar, ¾ tablespoons salt. Stir in ½ cup liquid shortening, 1 slightly beaten egg, and ½ cup milk. Stir until blended. Grease cookie sheet and drop batter in heaping tablespoons about 2 inches apart. Bake in 450° F oven for 12 to 15 minutes. Serve with your favorite berries and whipped cream.

RUM CHOCOLATE CAKE TOPPED AND LAYERED

POPCORN: 1¼ cups finely ground, 2 cups coarsely ground, and enough popped kernels for topping

Cream together ½ cup butter, 2 cups light brown sugar, and 1 teaspoon vanilla extract. Add 2 eggs. Mix well. Add ½ cup milk along with 1 cup flour, 1¼ cups finely ground popcorn, 1 teaspoon baking powder, a dash of salt, and 3 tablespoons cocoa mix. Mix well. Stir in 1 cup boiling water. Stir in 1 teaspoon rum extract. Pour into two 9 × 9–inch pans. Bake in 350° F oven for 50 minutes.

After layers are baked and cooled, slice each to make four thin layers. Thinly spread apricot jam on top of first layer. Then sprinkle with coarsely ground popcorn. Put on next layer of cake. Repeat the above, alternating apricot jam with cherry jam. When layers are in place, frost with whipped cream and refrigerate. Just before serving, sprinkle on a handful of popped popcorn.

POPCORN-NUT-DATE ROLL

POPCORN: ½ cup finely ground

Mix together one 8-ounce package of cream cheese and 1 cup melted butter. Stir in ½ cup finely ground popcorn and 1½ cups flour. Put mixture in refrigerator until firm. Remove and roll out dough about ⅛ inch thick on workboard sprinkled with powdered sugar. Cut dough in short strips, place some chopped nuts and dates on each and roll up. Place on greased cookie sheet and bake 10 to 15 minutes in 350° oven.

ORANGE-POPCORN TORTE

POPCORN: 1 cup finely ground

Combine 1 cup sugar and ½ cup melted butter. Mix in 2 egg yolks and ⅔ cup milk. Stir in 1 cup flour, 1 cup finely ground popcorn, and 2 teaspoons baking powder. Add 1 teaspoon vanilla, 2 tablespoons grated orange peel. Beat 2 egg whites, then fold into mixture. Pour into 9 × 9–inch baking pan and bake at 350° F for 50 mintues.

POPCORN-APPLE COBBLER

POPCORN: ½ cup finely ground

Melt 1 stick butter in 9-inch square baking dish. Mix well 1 cup sugar, ½ cup flour, ½ cup finely ground popcorn, 1½ teaspoons baking powder, ¾ teaspoon salt, and ¾ cup milk. Pour batter over melted butter. Arrange 4 cups peeled and sliced apples on top of batter. Bake at 350° F for 40 to 50 minutes, or until top is lightly browned.

PEACH AND POPCORN BUCKLE

POPCORN: ½ cup finely ground and 3 tablespoons coarsely ground

Mix together ½ cup sugar, 1 teaspoon baking powder, pinch of salt, ½ cup flour, and ½ cup finely ground popcorn. Stir in ⅓ cup soft butter and 2 eggs. Mix well and pour into greased and floured 9-inch square baking pan. Top with 1 can peach pie filling. Sprinkle on a mixture of ½ teaspoon cinnamon and 2 tablespoons sugar. Bake at 350° F for 40 minutes. Remove from oven and sprinkle 3 tablespoons coarsely ground popcorn on top, then return to oven for 10 minutes.

POPCORN FRUIT CUBES

POPCORN: ½ cup coarsely ground for recipe and 1½ cups coarsely ground for topping

Cream together ½ pound butter and 1 cup sugar. Add 1 teaspoon vanilla. Stir in 2 eggs, 1 at a time. Mix in well ½ cup coarsely ground popcorn, 1½ cups flour, and 1 cup chopped nuts. Pour ¾ mixture into ungreased 9 × 13–inch baking pan. Top with 1 can blueberry pie filling. Drizzle remaining mixture evenly over filling. Bake at 350° F for 45 minutes. Cool and sprinkle with remaining coarsely ground popcorn.

CHOCOLATE-POPCORN PIE

POPCORN: 4 cups

Mix together in a large saucepan 1¼ cups sugar, ½ cup powdered cocoa, a few drops of vinegar, and ¾ cup light corn syrup, a pinch of salt, and 2 tablespoons butter. Cook slowly over medium heat, stirring regularly. When sugar dissolves, bring to a boil, adding 2 tablespoons powdered milk, and ¼ cup water. Continue boiling until mixture reaches 250° F on a candy thermometer. Remove from heat and pour over 4 cups hot popcorn, coating evenly. Press ½ coated popcorn mixture into bottom of buttered deep pie plate. Add 1 cup chocolate chips. Top off with rest of coated popcorn and a few chocolate pieces. Spread on whipped cream topping. Slice and serve.

POPCORN-CHERRY-CHEESE DESSERT

POPCORN: ½ cup finely ground

Crush 20 graham cracker squares. Add ½ cup finely ground popcorn, ½ cup melted butter, and ½ cup sugar. Mix well and press into 9 × 13–inch cake pan. Beat together 4 eggs and two 8-ounce packages cream cheese. Add 1 cup sugar and 1½ teaspoons vanilla. Continue beating until smooth. Spread over mixture in pan and bake for 25 minutes at 325° F. Let cool and pour 1 can cherry pie filling on top. Chill and serve.

POPCORN CHOCOLATE MOUSSE

POPCORN: 2 cups coarsely ground and popped kernels for topping

Mix together 8 ounces whipped cream and 6 ounces chocolate syrup. Add ½ pound crushed chocolate chips and 2 cups coarsely ground popcorn. Stir well to combine, chill, and serve, topped with popcorn.

POPCORN-CHOCOLATE CREAM DESSERT

POPCORN: 4 cups

Melt 3½ ounces bitter chocolate in top of double boiler over hot water. Add 1¼ cups sugar and 1½ cups sour cream, stirring well. Bring water to boiling point, stirring contents of top pan for 8 minutes. Remove from heat and drizzle over 4 cereal bowls full of lightly buttered popcorn.

POPCORN-ORANGE-CHOCOLATE SAUCE

POPCORN: 2 cups coarsely ground

Mix together in top of a double boiler 1 cup chocolate syrup, ¼ cup condensed orange juice, and ½ cup finely grated orange rind, stirring constantly. Add 2 cups coarsely ground popcorn. Mix well. Drizzle over ice cream or cake.

POPCORN-CHOCOLATE SUNDAE TOPPING

POPCORN: about ½ cup coarsely ground

Melt 2 squares unsweetened chocolate and 2 tablespoons butter in saucepan over low heat. Mix in ½ cup evaporated milk and ⅔ cup sugar. Heat until thick. Add 1 teaspoon vanilla. Pour over a couple of scoops of your favorite ice cream. Sprinkle coarsely ground popcorn over the chocolate.

COOKIES

POPCORN COOKIES

POPCORN: 2 cups coarsely ground

Mix together 1 cup sugar, 2 cups coarsely ground popcorn, 2 cups flour, 1 teaspoon cinnamon, 1 teaspoon vanilla, and 1 egg yolk. Stir in 1 egg white beaten with 1 teaspoon sugar. Drop by spoonfuls on greased cookie sheet about 2 inches apart. Bake in 350° F oven for 15 minutes.

CHOCOLATE-POPCORN-RICE COOKIES

POPCORN: 3 cups coarsely ground

Heat 1 cup sugar and 1 cup light corn syrup over medium heat until boiling point. Remove and stir in 1 cup peanut butter. Add 4 cups Rice Krispies mixed with 3 cups coarsely ground popcorn. Mix and spread on greased 9 × 13–inch cake pan. Pour over 1 cup melted chocolate chips. Cool, cut, and serve.

POPCORN AND RICE KRISPIES CHEW

POPCORN: 2 cups coarsely ground

Melt ¼ pound butter and one 12-ounce package marshmallows in pan on low heat. Stirring constantly, boil for one minute and remove from heat. Mix together 4 cups Rice Krispies and 2 cups coarsely ground popcorn. Pour into large greased bowl. Drizzle on hot marshmallow mixture, fold and stir until well mixed. Spread in greased 9 × 13–inch cake pan. Let cool and cut into squares.

CHOCOLATE CHIP AND POPCORN COOKIES

POPCORN: 2 cups coarsely ground

Mix together 2 cups coarsely ground popcorn, 2 cups unsifted flour, 1 teaspoon baking soda, and pinch of salt. In separate bowl, cream together 1¼ cups butter, ½ cup sugar, ¾ cup brown sugar, and 1 teaspoon vanilla extract until smooth, then beat in 2 eggs. Combine both mixtures and sprinkle in one 12-ounce package chocolate chips. Drop by teaspoonful onto greased cookie sheet. Bake in 375° F oven for 8 to 10 minutes.

POPCORN-LEMON-ORANGE CRISPS

POPCORN: ¼ cup finely ground popcorn and ¾ cup coarsely ground popcorn

Cream together ½ cup sugar and ⅓ cup butter. Add 1 egg yolk, ¾ cup flour, ¼ cup finely ground popcorn, 1 finely grated orange rind, and 1 finely grated lemon rind. Mix well. Roll into small balls and dip in lightly beaten egg white and roll in ¾ cup chopped nuts and ¾ cup coarsely ground popcorn mixture. Put on greased cookie sheet and flatten a little with a fork. Bake in 350° F oven for 15 minutes.

POPCORN BROWNIES

POPCORN: ¼ cup finely ground

Cream together ½ cup butter and 1 cup sugar. Mix in 2 eggs and let stand. In a separate bowl, mix ¼ cup cocoa and a little water to make a paste. Combine mixtures. Stir in ¼ cup finely ground popcorn, ¾ cup flour, and ¼ cup milk. Add pinch of salt, 1 teaspoon vanilla, and ½ cup crushed nuts. Stir. Place in greased 9-inch square baking pan. Bake 20 minutes at 375° F. Remove from oven and dust with powdered sugar.

POPCORN TIE

POPCORN: 1 cup finely ground

Beat 11 egg yolks and blend in ½ pint sweet cream, 1 teaspoon salt. Pour mixture over 3 cups flour and 1 cup finely ground popcorn. Knead the dough until well mixed. Roll it out on a flat surface, lightly dusted with flour, until ⅛ inch thick. Cut rolled out dough in a diamond shape about 2 inches wide and 3 inches long. Then make a 1-inch-long cut through the middle of the widest part of the diamond and gently pull one point through slit in dough. Deep-fry in vegetable oil heated to 375° F. Remove and drain on paper towels. Sprinkle with white powdered sugar and finely ground popcorn.

BANG!

SNACKS

POPPED POPCORN AND PUFFED WHEAT CANDY

POPCORN: 4 cups

Heat ⅓ cup butter, ½ cup light corn syrup, and 2 tablespoons cocoa in saucepan over medium heat and bring to a rolling boil for about one minute. Stir in 1 teaspoon vanilla and remove from heat. Add 4 cups puffed wheat and 4 cups popcorn. Stir well to coat. Spread into greased 9 × 13–inch cake pan. Cool and cut into squares.

POPCORN–PEANUT BUTTER– COCONUT SNOWBALLS

POPCORN: 1 cup coarsely ground

Combine 1 cup finely chopped dates, 1 cup finely chopped walnuts, 1 cup coarsely ground popcorn, and 1½ cups peanut butter. Shape into small 1-inch balls. Make a thin icing with powdered sugar and two tablespoons cream. Spread a bit of icing on each popcorn ball and roll ball in coconut and coarsely ground popcorn, then serve.

POPCORN-RAISIN-NUT FUDGE CLUSTERS

POPCORN: ¾ cup

Combine ½ cup evaporated milk, ½ cup water, pinch of salt, 2 cups sugar in saucepan. Heat about 236° F. Melt ¼ cup butter over medium heat until brown, then add to mixture. Add 1 teaspoon vanilla. Let cool, then beat until creamy. Add ¾ cup nuts, ¾ cup raisins, and ¾ cup popcorn. Mix and drop by spoonful onto waxed paper.

POPCORN–ALMOND BUTTER-CRUNCH

POPCORN: 2 cups coarsely ground

Heat 1½ cups butter and 2 cups sugar over low heat, stirring until sugar is dissolved and syrup reaches 260° F. Add 1 cup sliced or slivered almonds and heat to 310° F, or the hard-crack stage. To test, drop a small amount of mixture into 1 cup of room-temperature water. If mixture turns hard immediately, it's ready. Pour out on lightly greased cookie sheet and let cool. Melt 12 ounces semisweet chocolate pieces and coat both sides of mixture, spreading evenly. Sprinkle with 2 cups coarsely ground popcorn. Cool and break up into small pieces.

MARSHMALLOW BALLS

POPCORN: 8 cups

Keep 8 cups popcorn warm in a 250° F oven. Melt 4 cups miniature marshmallows in large saucepan over low heat, stirring constantly. Add ½ cup butter, stirring until smooth. Pour mixture over popcorn, mixing until well covered. Add a handful of nuts, lightly salt, and shape into balls.

HONEYED POPCORN BALLS

POPCORN: 2 to 3 quarts

Keep 2 to 3 quarts popcorn warm in 250° oven. Heat 1½ cups honey until it reaches 250° F on a candy thermometer. Pour honey over popcorn. Mix until well covered. Let cool slightly and shape into balls.

CHOCOLATE POPCORN BALLS

POPCORN: 8 cups

Keep 8 cups popcorn warm in a 250° oven. Mix together in a large saucepan 1½ cups sugar, ½ cup light corn syrup, ½ cup water, ⅓ cup butter. Stir over medium heat until sugar melts and reaches candy stage (about 250° F). To test, drop a small amount of mixture into 1 cup room-temperature water. If mixture flattens out when it reaches bottom of the cup, it's ready. Remove popcorn from oven and stir in, mixing well to cover. Add 1½ cups chocolate chips. Mix and shape into balls.

CHOCOLATE-COVERED POPCORN

POPCORN: 8 cups

In top of double boiler melt 12 ounces chocolate chips, bitter or sweet. Stir constantly as chocolate melts. Lower heat when all is melted so it doesn't burn. Have ready 8 cups of popped corn. Pick the biggest kernels for chocolate covering. With two spoons take each kernel, drop in melted chocolate, and roll around until whole kernel is covered. Spoon kernel out of chocolate and place on waxed paper (don't let them touch). Refrigerate to cool and harden. They're ready to serve when chocolate is hard.

POPCORN-LEMON CUBES

POPCORN: 1 cup finely ground, ½ cup coarsely ground,
and 1½ cups coarsely ground for topping

Mix ½ pound soft butter, 1 cup flour, and 1 cup finely
ground popcorn. Press into 9 × 13–inch pan. Bake
at 400° F for 15 minutes. Prepare 2 packages lemon
pie filling (not instant) as directed on package. Into
warm crust sprinkle evenly 1 package miniature
marshmallows. Sprinkle ½ cup coarsely ground popcorn over marshmallows. Pour lemon mixture over
popcorn. Top with remaining coarsely ground popcorn and chill. Cube and serve.

POPCORN ICE CREAM

POPCORN: 1 cup coarsely ground

Beat 4 eggs, 2¼ cups sugar, 4½ teaspoons vanilla,
and 2 pinches of salt. Add 4 cups milk, 4 cups half-
and-half and beat. Add 1 cup coarsely ground popcorn, mixing well to coat. Pour into freezer can of
electric ice-cream maker. Follow manufacturer's directions. Makes 1 gallon, or 16 servings.

POPCORN-STRAWBERRY DELIGHT

POPCORN: 2½ cups coarsely ground

Cream together ½ pound butter and 2 cups powdered sugar. Crush 1 pound vanilla wafers and add to mixture. Press ⅔ of wafer mixture in 9-inch square baking pan. Lightly sprinkle 1 cup coarsely ground popcorn over wafers. In a bowl beat 2 eggs and 1 teaspoon vanilla for 15 minutes. Add to remaining ⅓ of wafer mixture and pour over wafers in pan. Slice 2 pints strawberries and place over mixture. Sprinkle 1 cup more coarsely ground popcorn on and top with whipped cream. Sprinkle ½ cup coarsely ground popcorn on top. Put in refrigerator to cool.

POPCORN-PINEAPPLE-MARSH-MALLOW DELIGHT

POPCORN: 3 cups coarsely ground

Melt 1 pound marshmallows in ¼ cup milk in sauce-pan over low heat, stirring constantly. Remove from heat and cool. Mix in 1 small can crushed pineapple with juice and 1 pint of whipping cream. Mix 3 cups of crushed graham crackers and 3 cups coarsely ground popcorn. Press cracker and popcorn mixture in bottom of pan. Save a little to sprinkle for topping. Pour filling over crumbs and refrigerate for 3 hours.

POPCORN-CHOCOLATE-ALMOND-HONEY SAUCE

POPCORN: ¼ cup coarsely ground

Melt 4 ounces bitter chocolate in top of double boiler over hot water. Add ¾ cup honey and mix until smooth. Stir in ¼ cup slivered almonds and ¼ cup coarsely ground popcorn. Remove from heat and driz-zle over lightly buttered popcorn, mixing well.

POPCORN FUDGE

POPCORN: 1 cup coarsely ground

Mix together 4 cups miniature marshmallows, ⅔ cup evaporated milk, ¼ cup butter, and 1½ cups sugar in a saucepan. Bring to a boil and cook over medium heat for five minutes, stirring often. Remove from heat, add 12 ounces chocolate chips and 1 teaspoon vanilla. When chocolate is melted, add 1 cup coarsely ground popcorn. Mix to coat well. Pour into lightly buttered 9 × 9–inch baking pan and chill.

POPCORN-CARAMEL TREATS

POPCORN: 1 cup coarsely ground

Melt 16 ounces caramels with 3 tablespoons heavy dairy cream in top of double boiler, stirring often. Mix together in large bowl 1 cup granola cereal, 1 cup crispy rice cereal, 1 cup shredded coconut, 1 cup chopped nuts, and 1 cup coarsely ground popcorn. Drizzle caramel mixture over dry mixture and mix thoroughly so as to cover evenly. Drop by tablespoonsful onto waxed paper.

PEANUT BUTTER AND JELLY POPCORN

POPCORN: 8 cups

Mix 2 tablespoons melted butter, 2 tablespoons crunchy peanut butter, and 2 tablespoons strawberry jelly in saucepan over low heat. Slice 1 pint of strawberries, and add to popcorn along with ½ cup peanuts. Toss well to combine. Pour peanut butter and jelly mixture over popcorn, mixing thoroughly.

POPCORN-CHOCOLATE PEANUT BUTTER

POPCORN: 8 cups

In a large saucepan over low heat, mix together 1 cup sugar, ⅓ cup corn syrup, ⅓ cup water, ¼ cup butter, and pinch of salt. Stir until sugar melts. Cook and bring to boil stirring constantly until mixture reaches 250° F on a candy thermometer. Remove from heat and pour over hot popcorn and mix well. Butter 2 large loaf pans and press a 1-inch layer of popcorn in bottom. Then spread a layer of peanut butter. Then add another layer of coated popcorn. Sprinkle a layer of chocolate chips on top. Place in a 250° oven for 5 minutes until chocolate starts to melt. Remove from oven. Cool and slice.

POPCORN HAWAIIAN LEI

POPCORN: 20 cups

Mix together in large saucepan 2 cups sugar, 1½ cups water, pinch of salt, ½ cup light corn syrup, 1 teaspoon vinegar. Cook until hard-ball stage, or 250° F on a candy thermometer. To test, drop small amount of mixture into 1 cup room-temperature water. If mixture turns hard and stiff immediately, it's ready. Then add 1 teaspoon vanilla, 5 quarts hot popcorn, ½ grated orange peel, ½ cup candied pineapple, ½ cup quartered and drained maraschino cherries, and 1 cup shredded coconut. Pour hot candy mixture over popcorn, coating evenly. On a large platter or tray, mold the mixture into a large oval shape (hole in the middle). Decorate with more fruit if you wish and serve.

POPCORN-FUDGE ROCKY ROAD

POPCORN: 3 cups

Melt five 4½-ounce chocolate bars in top of double boiler over medium heat. Remove from heat and beat smooth. Add 3 cups miniature marshmallows and 3 cups popcorn. Mix well and pour into buttered baking pan. Chill and cut into squares when firm.

POPCORN SNOWBALLS

POPCORN: 1½ cups coarsely ground

Mix together in top of double boiler over medium heat one 6-ounce package (1 cup) chocolate pieces and ⅓ cup evaporated milk. As chocolate melts, blend until smooth then remove from heat. Stir in 1 cup powdered sugar and ½ cup coarsely ground popcorn. Mix well. Let cool and form into small balls and roll in 1 cup coarsely ground popcorn. Makes about 20 balls.

POPCORN CRUNCH

POPCORN: 3 cups

Mix together in a large saucepan over medium heat 1⅓ cups sugar, 1 cup butter, 1 tablespoon light corn syrup, and 3 tablespoons water. Heat and stir to crack stage, about 300° F on a candy thermometer. To test, drop small amount of mixture into 1 cup room-temperature water. If mixture turns hard immediately, it's ready. Quickly stir in 3 cups hot popcorn. Spread out in greased 9 × 13–inch cake pan and cool. When hard, break apart in pieces and serve.

POPCORN CLUSTERS

POPCORN: 2½ cups

Melt one 8-ounce package chocolate pieces in top of double boiler over hot water. Stir in 2½ cups popcorn. Drop by spoonsful onto waxed paper or cookie sheet. Chill and serve.

POPCORN—PEANUT BUTTER ROLL-UP

POPCORN: 2½ cups coarsely ground

Mix together 1 cup peanut butter and 1 cup powdered sugar. Beat in 2 tablespoons dark molasses. Mix in 1 cup coarsely ground popcorn. Divide mixture in half and roll into two 1-inch-thick rolls. Roll in remaining coarsely ground popcorn. Wrap in waxed paper. Cool and slice.

POPCORN-CHOCOLATE SQUARES

POPCORN: ¼ cup finely ground and ½ cup coarsely ground

Mix ¾ cup flour and ¼ cup finely ground popcorn, ½ cup butter, 2 tablespoons sugar, and ½ cup chopped nuts. Press into a greased and floured 9-inch square pan. Bake at 375° F for 15 minutes, then let cool. Mix one 8-ounce package cream cheese, 1 cup powdered sugar, 1 cup prepared whipped cream, and ½ cup coarsely ground popcorn. Pour on crust. In a bowl, pour 3 cups milk and 2 small packages of instant chocolate pudding mix and beat until thick. Pour this mixture over cream mixture already on crust. Top with prepared whipped cream and ½ cup coarsely ground popcorn and refrigerate overnight. Cut into squares.

BUTTERED CANDY BAR POPCORN

POPCORN: 8 cups

In top of double boiler melt one 16-ounce package vanilla caramels over hot water. Add 4 tablespoons butter and mix well. Drizzle over 8 cups popcorn and stir to cover evenly. Sprinkle pecans on mixture and dust with powdered sugar. Mix again and pour out on waxed paper or cookie sheet to form bars about 2 × 3 inches. Cool and serve.

GERMAN CHOCOLATE POPCORN

POPCORN: 8 cups

Melt 2¾ cups semisweet chocolate chips in top of double boiler over hot water. Stir in ½ cup light corn syrup, 2 tablespoons brown sugar, 3 tablespoons butter. Drizzle over hot popcorn and stir to cover evenly. Sprinkle ¾ cup shredded coconut and ¾ cup crushed nuts over and mix again. Let cool slightly and serve.

POPCORN-CAROB CRUNCH

POPCORN: 2 cups

Mix together 2 cups popcorn, ½ cup sunflower seeds, ½ cup peanuts, 1 cup raisins, 1 cup carob chips.

POPCORN–PEANUT BUTTER– BANANA BALLS

POPCORN: 8 cups

Mix together in large saucepan 1½ cups light corn syrup and 1½ cups peanut butter. When mixture starts to boil, blend well and remove from heat. Pour mixture over 8 cups hot popcorn and 1 cup dehydrated banana chips. Mix well to coat evenly and shape into balls.

POP
THE QUESTION

And there they sat, a-popping corn,
    John Styles and Susan Cutter—
John Styles as fat as any ox,
    And Susan fat as butter.

And there they sat and shelled the corn,
    And raked and stirred the fire,
And talked of different kinds of corn,
    And hitched their chairs up tighter.

Then Susan she the popper shook,
    Then John he shook the popper,
Till both their faces grew as red
    As saucepans made of copper.

And then they shelled, and popped, and ate,
    All kinds of fun a-poking,
While he haw-hawed at her remarks,
    And she laughed at his joking.

And still they popped, and still they ate—
    John's mouth was like a hopper—
And stirred the fire, and sprinkled salt,
    And shook and shook the popper.

The clock struck nine—the clock struck ten,
    And still the corn kept popping;
It struck eleven, and then struck twelve,
    And still no signs of stopping.

And John he ate, and Sue she thought—
    The corn did pop and patter—
Till John cried out, "The corn's a-fire!
    Why, Susan, what's the matter?"

Said she, "John Styles, it's one o'clock;
    You'll die of indigestion;
I'm sick of all this popping corn—
    Why don't you pop the question?"

—Anonymous, in *The World's Best Poetry*,
    The University Society, 1904

ABOUT THE AUTHOR

Robert Brucken is an artist, painter, sculptor, and author. He was educated at the Columbus College of Art and Design and has worked in advertising for eighteen years. He lives in Upper Arlington, Ohio, with his wife, Mickey, and son, Alix. Bob has always loved popcorn. He wrote *Bang!* for people who share his love.